An opinionated guide to

MARSEILLE

Written by
SANDRINE FAURE

Tuba Club (no.57)

INFORMATION IS DEAD.
LONG LIVE OPINION.

When we conceived these guidebooks, we feared they would fail. Who needs a guidebook when everything can be googled for free?

But then it occurred to us: that's exactly why you *do* want a guidebook. You want lively, trustworthy opinion combined with great photographs. You don't want endless information from a thousand online bots.

We think you are like us: you care about quality, you care about style, you care about provenance, but you don't have time to waste on long words like 'provenance'. You want to cut to the chase: where's good?

We are an independent from London. How dare we write a book about Marseille? Because we work with passionate local writers who seek out the spots that remind us of the east London we know and love: these are the most creative, diverse and exciting places of all.

Ann & Martin, co-founders
Hoxton Mini Press

FORUS
Coiffure
MASCULINE

Mucem (no.42)
Opposite: Limmat (no.2)

Île Degaby (no.13)

Opposite: Provisions (no.34)

Parc National des Calanques (no.54)

SORRY, PARIS

I moved to Marseille from Paris when I was five, which meant I spent my childhood fielding the ultimate football question: PSG or OM? I learned fast to give the right answer. But for years, I barely knew the city. We lived far away from the centre, and Marseille is vast – a collection of 111 villages rather than a single city – so I often went weeks without seeing the centre, or even the sea. And I resented the Mistral, the infamous wind of Provence. Days when its fierce, freezing gusts rattled the shutters and emptied the streets felt like a punishment. When I left for university in Paris, I thought I was done with Marseille. But distance does funny things. It wasn't until I started coming back as a visitor that everything clicked.

The city was changing too. Marseille was declared the 2013 European Capital of Culture, which brought the Mucem (no.42) and a wave of investment that reconnected the city to its waterfront. I started walking neighbourhoods I'd barely known: the sensory chaos of Noailles, where you can lose an hour in Maison Empereur (no.29) or browse the crammed shelves at Jiji La Palme d'Or (no.38). I rediscovered Saint-Victor, following my favourite scent in the world – orange blossom biscuits – to Le Four des Navettes (no.9). I wandered the winding streets of Endoume and fell for Frioul (no.53), the scrappy offshore islands that most visitors never see. Somewhere along the line, I stopped saying I was from Paris.

Marseille isn't without contradictions. The gap between the grand villas of Le Roucas-Blanc and the northern *cités* – built to house waves of workers from the former colonies, then left to decay as industries disappeared – is real and stark. It feeds the reputation you've probably heard: France's most dangerous city, a place to avoid. But the reality is messier and far more interesting. Marseille has always been France's gateway to the Mediterranean, which means it's never been entirely French. It feels more like Naples than Lyon – a city that looks south across the sea rather than north towards Paris. You hear it in the Arabic mixed with the Provençal accent, taste it in the food at Chez Yassine (no.11) and Bistrot Baya (no.15) and see it in the fact that this 2,600-year-old port has absorbed everyone who ever washed up on its shores.

The food scene reflects that same energy. It reveres the classics – a good bouillabaisse is non-negotiable – but it has expanded to include a new guard of chefs. The pizza trucks – a Marseille invention from the '60s – like Chez Gé (no.25) remain neighbourhood institutions, but now they share the city with Paul Langlère's bistronomy at Sépia (no.1) and the guest chefs at La Ola (no.12). At Limmat (no.2), you eat incredible market food on the terrace above Cours Julien, while at Mercato (no.68), the natural wine flows as freely as the football debates.

And then there's the sea. It's the reason we're all here. Whether you're hiking the white cliffs of the Calanques (no.54) or eating panisses at L'Estaque (no.49) in the north, the Mediterranean frames everything. You can be diving off the rocks at Malmousque (no.56) or having lunch at the edge of the map at La Marine des Goudes (no.6), and suddenly the traffic fades into the distance. Out here, I have finally made peace with the Mistral; the wind is the price you pay for the light. These are the moments that define Marseille – not the postcards or the headlines. This guide is here to show you where to find them. And if anyone asks? *Allez l'OM.*

Sandrine Faure
Marseille, 2026

Sandrine Faure writes about travel, food and all the destinations she can reach by train. A former editor of *Metropolitan*, Eurostar's magazine, she grew up in Marseille before moving to London in her twenties. She returns often, lured by the hum of art spaces hidden in old factories, cult pizza vans and warm navettes (in no particular order). She can be found on Instagram at @sandrineccfaure.

HOW TO NAVIGATE
THE CITY

Marseille is vast – geographically twice the size of Paris – having grown by swallowing up surrounding villages. This history defines how you navigate: the centre is dense and walkable (though the hills around Endoume, Vauban and Notre-Dame de la Garde will test your calves), but reaching the outlying spots requires a plan. Cycling is tough here – it's regularly voted France's worst city for bikes – and the traffic in Marseille makes driving a headache, so skip the rental car unless you plan on exploring the wider Provence region.

Instead, use the RTM network (bus, metro, tram). The metro runs until 12:30am Thursday–Saturday (9:30pm the rest of the week) and the tram runs until 12:30am every day. Locals joke that the tram just covers the same stops as the metro, and they're not completely wrong, but at least you get a view. In summer, the best travel hack is the boat shuttle (La Navette) which runs along the coast from the Vieux-Port to L'Estaque and Pointe Rouge. For late nights or longer treks, traditional taxis are easier to find than they used to be, and apps like Uber and Bolt are now everywhere. Like any big city, it's wise to stay street-smart at night.

For the spots outside that are trickier to access, we've added specific 'Getting there' tips.

A PERFECT WEEKEND

Friday night

Check in at Hôtel Amista (no.61) in the heart of Noailles then head for the city's best sunset ritual at Le Café de l'Abbaye (no.66). Watch the sky turn orange over the port before walking up the hill for dinner. Sépia (no.1) offers incredible bistronomy with views over the city garden or, for something buzzier, try the packed terrace at La Relève (no.69).

Saturday morning

Dive straight into the energy outside your hotel door. Fuel up with coffee and a croissant at Pétrin Couchette (no.10) then get lost in the aisles of Maison Empereur (no.29) and the spice jars of Jiji La Palme d'Or (no.38).

Saturday lunch

Cross town to Le Panier for a Marseille rite of passage: pizza at Chez Étienne (no.19). It's loud, cash-only and covered in celebrity photos – and serves the best anchovy pizza in the city.

Saturday afternoon

Walk off lunch by exploring the Mucem (no.42), crossing the high-wire footbridge to Fort Saint-Jean. From there, wander up to Le Panier to see the peaceful courtyard of La Vieille Charité (no.44) and grab a coffee in the sun in the on-site cafe, OLLā.

Saturday evening

Head to Cours Julien for the city's best nightlife. Book a table at Livingston (no.3) for creative small plates, then squeeze into Mercato (no.68) for natural wine under the football scarves. Afterwards, jump in a cab to Le Chapiteau (no.67) for an open-air party or to La Dame Noir (no.71) by the port.

Sunday morning

Take a pilgrimage to Le Corbusier's Cité Radieuse (no.41) – a utopian housing estate of 'streets in the sky'. Visit the MAMO art centre on the roof and see why this vertical village is still a masterpiece of modernism.

Sunday lunch

Go all the way to the end of the world: the fishing village of Les Goudes. Lunch at La Marine des Goudes (no.6) feels a million miles from the city, despite being just a 30-minute drive away – or try Tuba (no.57) next door.

Sunday afternoon

Spend the rest of the day in nature. Hike the Calanques (no.54) coastal trails that start nearby or, in summer, visit the sculpture park at Friche de l'Escalette (no.45). On the way back to town, stop for a final swim at Malmousque (no.56).

Sunday evening

Marseille is famously sleepy on Sunday nights but Chez Yassine (no.11) stays open. End the weekend here with a steaming bowl of Tunisian soup and the city's best atmosphere.

1
SÉPIA

Bistronomy with a view

Paul Langlère never stops. The Marseille-born chef behind Cécile Food Club (no.5) and La Marine des Goudes (no.6) took over a snack bar on the Puget hill in 2017, redefining Marseille bistronomy in the process. The dining room looks out over the city and sea, and his plates reflect the harbour below – smoked mackerel or anchovies – even when meat is the main event. The siphon chocolate mousse has been on the menu since day one, and for good reason – it's one of the best things you'll eat in Marseille. If you're not in the mood for a full meal, slip next door to Julis, where barman Lulu mixes cocktails on the terrace.

2 rue Vauvenargues, 13007
Nearest metro: Estrangin
restaurant-sepia.fr

SÉPI

2
LIMMAT

Lilian's market kitchen

Lilian Gadola swapped Zürich for Marseille in 2017, opening Limmat on the painted steps between Cours Julien and Noailles. The menu is short and changes with the market – one fish dish, one vegetarian option, whatever's good that week. Sweet potato tarte tatin one day, squid and leek pancakes the next, and perhaps stuffed sardines with tomato semolina when they're at their best. And if you're lucky enough to visit in winter, she sometimes runs soirée fondue nights that sell out the moment she announces them on Instagram. It's a tight squeeze inside, so book ahead.

41 rue Jean-Baptiste-Estelle, 13006
Nearest metro: Notre-Dame du Mont
limmatmarseille.com

3

LIVINGSTON

Chef residencies done right

What chef and co-founder Valentin Raffali started as ambitious small plates has morphed into one of Marseille's most exciting dining experiments: visiting chefs taking over the kitchen for months at a time, each bringing their own '3 rounds' (three-course) vision. The results? Unpredictable, often brilliant and always worth the gamble – whether that's betel-wrapped lamb, fried mussels or a more casual pizza pop-up. The space perfectly matches the Cours Julien energy – buzzing with the neighbourhood's restaurant-hopping crowd, relaxed enough that you won't feel underdressed, but serious about what lands on your plate. Book ahead, or risk disappointment when the latest culinary star sells out their residency.

5 rue Crudère, 13006
Nearest metro: Notre-Dame du Mont
livingstonmarseille.com

ED
BCR
RUE
VIAN
ET SI TU
DOIS GARDER
LE SECRET
École
mondiale du
COMMUNISME
Tenace
Hundred eyes
OUI!

4

POISSONNERIE KENNEDY

The Corniche's seafood hotspot

Marseille entrepreneur Christophe Juville has a knack for spotting a good corner. This time, he's taken a historic fishmonger on the Corniche coastal road and turned it into one of Malmousque's busiest tables. Poissonnerie Kennedy keeps it simple: fresh seafood, grilled fish and natural wine. The setting is minimal, with a tiled counter inside and tables lining the pavement outside. It's loud, energetic and serves some of the best oysters in town. Don't come for a quiet dinner; come to eat impeccable seafood in the thick of it.

245 Corniche Président John Fitzgerald Kennedy, 13007
Nearest bus stop: Fausse Monnaie (line 83)
poissonneriekennedy.com

5

CÉCILE FOOD CLUB

The Corniche cafe with a queue

The queues at this cafe, deli and caterer above the tiny fishing village of Malmousque haven't let up since it opened in 2023. If you're lucky, they'll have the pan bagnat – essentially a niçoise salad inside wholewheat bread. With proper chunks of tuna, eggs and anchovies in a bap that somehow stays soft when soaked in olive oil, this is Marseille's best version of the sandwich. Or look out for their veggie kebab: celeriac cooked and spiced so well you'll forget about meat. Grab whatever you're having and head down to the rocks below – eating lunch with your feet dangling in the Mediterranean is the whole point.

116 Corniche Président John Fitzgerald Kennedy, 13007
Nearest bus stop: Endoume (line 83)
ceciledeli.com

Cécile
FOOD CLUB MALMOUSQUE
116 CORNICHE KENNEDY

6

LA MARINE DES GOUDES

Seafood at the end of the world

If you're keeping score, yes, this is Paul Langlère's third entry in the guide. After Sépia (no.1) in the city centre and Cécile (no.5) on the Corniche, he and partner Thibault Hillmeyer have headed for the end of the world. This harbourfront spot in Les Goudes brings the same sharp, ingredient-led cooking to a seaside setting. The bouillabaisse is exceptional and surprisingly affordable, but the daily catch rules the menu. Don't overlook the pasta dishes and definitely save room for the chocolate mousse – it will stay with you long after you leave.

16 rue Désiré Pélaprat, 13008
Getting there: car/taxi recommended
la-marine-des-goudes-restaurant-marseille.com

BAR
RESTAURANT
LA MARINE
SPÉCIALITÉS
MARSEILLAISES
Bouillabaisse
Retour de Pointu
RESTAURANT
LA MARINE
BAR
LA MARINE

7

OUREA

The open kitchen favourite

Since 2018, Matthieu Roche (pictured overleaf) and Camille Fromont have been running this quietly brilliant restaurant tucked behind the Palais de Justice, where French classics get a nudge in new directions – bonito carpaccio is served with vanilla oil, and the choux pastry comes with pecan and pear. The room is small, with green sofas and mirrors catching the light from the open kitchen, where someone always seems to be zesting citrus or whisking something at the pass. The menu changes weekly with the market's best and plates land fast, still warm from the stove. Come for lunch – €35 gets you the full trio – and you'll understand why this place has such a devoted following.

72 rue de la Paix Marcel Paul, 13006
Nearest metro: Estrangin
ourea-restaurant.com

8

CATERINE

The neighbourhood canteen

Marseillais have been loving this neighbourhood eatery since it was opened by Marie Dijon and her two co-owners mid-pandemic. There's no table service here: order at the counter and pick up your tray. It's just €27 for the full menu, a reasonable price for a seasonally changing roster of dishes that might include stuffed courgette flowers, oysters with dried pork and kumquat or Marie's famous octopus kebab. On warm days, grab a seat in the courtyard out back. If it's full, or the weather turns, you'll end up at a big table inside, sharing space with strangers who'll probably become friends by dessert.

27 rue Fontange, 13006
Nearest metro: Notre-Dame du Mont
instagram.com/caterine.mrs

Tous nos
vins
sont
à emporter
(+10%)
LAROUSSE
des DESSERTS
L'AFRIQUE

9

LE FOUR DES NAVETTES

Scents of the city

Forget petrichor or freshly cut grass. In Marseille, the winning scent comes from Le Four des Navettes – a rich mix of dough and orange blossom that hits you from streets away. These boat-shaped biscuits split locals: some moan they're too dry, but they're wrong. Since 1781, this bakery near Saint-Victor Abbey has been making navettes the same way, blessed every Candlemas by the archbishop himself. The bags are almost as lovely as what's inside – perfect for keeping in the kitchen long after the biscuits are gone.

136 rue Sainte, 13007
Nearest metro: Estrangin
fourdesnavettes.com

J. Claude Imbert
Maître Artisan
FOUR DES NAVETTES
136, RUE SAINTE
13007 MARSEILLE
Tél. 04 91 33 32 12   FAX 04 91 33 65 69
e-mail : contact@fourdesnavettes.com
internet : fourdesnavettes.com
MÉDAILLE d'OR Exposition Internationale de PARIS 1900
PATRIMOINE NATIONAL DES SPECIALITES DE FRANCE 1994
OSCAR de FRANCE de L'ARTISANAT 1999
PRIX de la DYNAMIQUE ARTISANALE 2000
PRIX de L'IMAGE de MARSEILLE 2004
Exclusivité de fabrication

10

PÉTRIN COUCHETTE

Marseille's coffee-and-bread favourite

Just off Noailles, this bakery–cafe from the Small Group crew (see Livingston, no.3) has turned the corner spot into something special: proper sourdough bread, excellent coffee and sandwiches worth crossing town for. Their tagline says it all: 'pain vivant & café délicieux' (lively bread and delicious coffee) – and they're not lying. Skip the morning rush and come for lunch when that sunny terrace fills up, and make sure to order the egg sandwich if it's on the menu that day. The coffee's worth lingering over, too – the team behind that bright yellow counter pulls perfect shots. Oh, and pick up a loaf for tomorrow's breakfast before you leave.

7 Cours Saint-Louis, 13001
Nearest metros: Noailles, Vieux-Port
petrincouchette.com

11

CHEZ YASSINE

Tunisian soup perfection

Marseille loves a good soup, but this Noailles institution stands out on the bustling rue d'Aubagne. The family-run team behind the counter know their way around chickpeas, harissa and the perfect amount of olive oil. Don't expect fancy decor – you're here for the food. The leblebi, a North African chickpea stew, arrives steaming hot with bread that soaks up the spiced broth beautifully. Still hungry? Try the fricassé, a savoury pastry filled with tuna, eggs and plenty of flavour. Come at 2pm when the lunch rush ebbs or join the regulars who've made late afternoon soup their daily ritual.

8a rue d'Aubagne, 13001
Nearest metro: Noailles
chezyassine.com

CHEZ
Yassine

12

LA OLA

The kitchen carousel

Opened by Andréa Pittaluga in 2023, the kitchen at La Ola is helmed by a rotating cast of chefs. Ely Tran cooked there recently, drawing on her Vietnamese and Laotian roots for dishes like Oua Si Koong (stuffed lemongrass with prawn), or chè (Vietnamese sweet soup) with pandan spaghetti, strawberries and kiwi. Before her, Margaux Fary turned out beef cheek croquettes with Phu Quoc pepper alongside those famous Soissons beans in spiced broth. Andréa's front-of-house team is all-women, the natural wine list is strong and the menu changes with whoever's in residence.

12 rue Vian, 13006
Nearest metro: Notre-Dame du Mont
instagram.com/laola.marseille

13
ÎLE DEGABY

Dinner on a forbidden island

For years, this island was off-limits – a Louis XIV fort you could swim past but never enter. Now, chefs Sébastien Dugast and Romain Nicoli run a seasonal restaurant and bar here from April to November. A boat ride delivers you to a fortress where Mediterranean sharing plates and local seafood are served against an unbeatable backdrop. Between courses, you're free to swim off the rocks or wander the old fort's grounds. It feels illicit, like you've snuck into someone's private domain – just be sure to book well in advance.

Île Degaby, 13007
Getting there: ferry from quai de l'Anse de Maldormé;
book via website
iledegaby.com

14

BISTROT SASSY

DJ nights and œuf mayo

Bistrot Sassy sits on boulevard Chave, right by the tram, and lives up to its name and its motto: insolence. The bright blue tables are the first sign that this place doesn't play by the rules. Take the classics: the œuf mayo is upgraded with a hit of black garlic and shiitake reduction that makes it rich and deeply savoury. The cocktails are strong and the bar snacks hold their own – like molten goat cheese arancini and a fermented chilli ketchup with a real kick. On weekends, a DJ often sets up and the whole place shifts from bistro to party without anyone batting an eye.

167 boulevard Chave, 13005
Nearest metro: La Timone
instagram.com/bistrot_sassy

15

BISTROT BAYA

Cooking her way home

Named after owner Maeva Hocini's Algerian grandmother, Bistrot Baya serves 'cuisine de l'exil' (exile cooking) – food that pulls from her Kabyle and Arab roots while staying seasonal and Provençal. The asbanes (stuffed lamb intestines) come with Jerusalem artichoke purée, hazelnuts, braised veal and mushroom duxelle – a decadent twist on this traditional dish. The restaurant has two rooms, one of them an art gallery, and Maeva brings in visiting chefs for residencies now and then – check who's cooking before you book.

23 boulevard National, 13001
Nearest metros: Réformés Canebière,
Marseille Saint-Charles
instagram.com/bistrot.baya

BOUILLABAISSE TURFU

The seafood stew you can actually afford

Bouillabaisse – Marseille's famous saffron-laced fish stew – usually costs €60–100 at the classic spots. Christian Qui does it differently, championing Mediterranean biodiversity one affordable bowl at a time. His tiny counter near the Vieux-Port serves street-food bouillabaisse for under €10, built on that morning's catch. He's there at dawn, passionate about forgotten fish and sustainable catches. When the Mistral blows too hard and the fishermen stay in, he closes too. The caveat? In this windy city, he's closed as often as he's open. Call ahead or risk finding the shutters down.

1 rue Pythéas, 13001
Nearest metro: Vieux-Port
instagram.com/bouillabaisse_turfu

BOUILLABAISSE
TURFU

17
BOULANGERIE MERLIN

Bread magic

Marseille's bakeries are hit or miss – some great, some overpriced and underwhelming. Boulangerie Merlin, just off La Plaine, is one of the best. Run by three brothers from a baking family, the sign out front explains that 'bread connects us' – and yes, you'll feel the connection. Get the focaccia or the pizzette with homemade tomato sauce and feta or grab a petit pain au chocolat for 50 cents. There's a trestle table, an oven behind the counter and that's about it – you'll probably see your bread coming out while you're choosing. They close for a three-hour lunch (why wouldn't you?), so check the time before you go.

94 rue Saint-Savournin, 13001
Nearest metro: Réformés Canebière
instagram.com/boulangerie_merlin

RUE
SAINT-SAVOURNIN
Merlin
• BOULANGERIE •
M
Le Pain
C'est
le lien
Pain au
Levain
Fait à la
Main
OUVERT

18

SUR LE POUCE

Marseille's couscous obsession

Ask the French what their favourite dish is, and couscous often tops the list. In Marseille, that love runs deeper. Sur le Pouce in Belsunce has been serving Tunisian couscous for over 40 years, and locals will argue it's the best in the city. The lamb shank is what keeps them coming back – slow-cooked with garlic and spices until you can pull it apart with a spoon, the meat soft and rich. The grains arrive fluffy on one plate, the sauce on another, thick with chickpeas and vegetables that have been simmering for hours.

2 rue des Convalescents, 13001
Nearest metros: Colbert, Noailles
instagram.com/resto_surlepouce

Sur le pouce
SUR LE POUCE
PLATS DU JOUR
CUISINE
ORIENTALE

19

CHEZ ÉTIENNE

How Marseille does pizza

Marseillais take pizza seriously. There are the trucks (see Chez Gé, no.25), the boulangerie slices – and then there's Chez Étienne, which has been around so long (since 1943), it's become part of the old Le Panier quarter. Three generations have run this spot, and the brown shopfront hasn't changed in decades. Inside, it's loud and packed, with photos of celebrities who have eaten here covering every wall. The pizza menu comes down to two choices: cheese (Emmental, of course) or anchovies, both fired in a wood-burning oven that gives them a thin, perfectly blistered crust. Don't forget to start with supions – fried squid with garlic and parsley that locals order every time. Bring cash.

43 rue de Lorette, 13002
Nearest metro: Colbert

PIZZARIA
ETIENNE

20

LA CANTINETTA

Italian done right

In Marseille, Italian food is everywhere, for better or worse. At La Cantinetta, it's certainly for the best. Inside, elegant white tablecloths stand out against dark walls lined with wood panelling. The classics are spot on, too – the cacio e pepe bursts with the right amount of pepper (and cheese). If the weather's pleasant, head for the courtyard, where the terracotta's wonky and the tree feels like it's been there longer than the restaurant. Come for a long, leisurely lunch with a bottle of Montepulciano or claim a table for a summertime dinner when the evening air finally cools.

24 Cours Julien, 13006
Nearest metros: Noailles, Notre-Dame du Mont
restaurantlacantinetta.fr

21

PROSPER

The instant classic

This might be the hardest table to book off Cours Julien, but it's worth the effort. True to the vision of owners François Roche and Santiago Michel, this bistrot–trattoria feels more like someone's great dinner party: tortilla with green harissa and spicy mayo, morel pasta that disappears too fast, pizza fritta with melting taleggio. The wine list leans natural, mostly composed of French and Argentine bottles, with Archipel kombucha if you're taking a night off. Six months after opening in early 2025, they landed in the Michelin Guide. Turns out it really is the best dinner party in town.

2 rue des Trois Rois, 13006
Nearest metro: Notre-Dame du Mont
instagram.com/prosper.marseille

22
AU CONTRAIRE PÂTISSERIE

Breaking pastry conventions

Walk into Au Contraire, and you'll think you've stumbled into a '70s dream – it's all orange and yellow retro charm in the lively Vauban neighbourhood. The lemon and hazelnut tart has sharp citrus balanced with nutty praline, the pistachio and orange blossom tart is rich and floral, and the vanilla flan wobbles perfectly. Here's the twist: none of it contains refined sugar. Marie-Luce Grisoli convinced her mother to retrain as a pâtissière, and in 2019 they opened this place to prove healthy doesn't mean boring. Can you tell the difference? Absolutely not. It's worth the climb, especially if someone's told you to watch your sugar.

1 boulevard Paul Doumer, 13006
Nearest metro: Estrangin
aucontrairepatisserie.com

AU CONTRAIRE

23

CHEZ PETIT JEAN

The Irano-Corsican counter

This tiny grocery in the increasingly hip Camas neighbourhood belongs to Kiana (Iranian) and Vincent Colonna (Corsican), and it shows on the shelves: Corsican charcuterie sits alongside spices and products from Iran. That fusion makes its way into the sandwiches – brousse cheese gets a citrusy hit from Iranian dried lemon, while smoky figatelli (Corsican pork liver sausage) is balanced by saffron's floral warmth. You can grab a sandwich to go, linger over a cheeseboard and wine at the little tables outside or just shop the shelves and cook for yourself.

65 boulevard Eugène Pierre, 13005
Nearest metro: Noailles
instagram.com/chez_petijean

SANDWICHERIE

24
CHEZ MOE

Moe's double act

The historic quarter of Le Panier has been filling up with new spots lately, and Chez Moe on Grand Rue is one of them. It's the kind of place where you pop in for morning coffee and somehow find yourself back that evening with a glass of wine. Moe – Mohcène Zaïgouche, Marseille-born with an improbable tech background and years spent travelling – has figured out the formula: Möka coffee and cardamom brioche when you need it, natural wine when you want it, all in a small space with light wood and a terrace that fills up fast.

38 Grand Rue, 13002
Nearest metros: Colbert, Vieux-Port
instagram.com/chezmoe

chez moi
chez moi

25

PIZZA TRUCK CHEZ GÉ

Chez Gé's moitié-moitié

Talk to a Marseillais about pizza trucks and watch them puff up with pride. They invented them, after all – in 1962, Jean Meritan loaded a wood-burning oven onto a trailer and kicked off something that's still going strong. Now, trucks park up across the city, queues forming most nights. Chez Gé, on boulevard de la Blancarde, is one of the best: proper Marseille pizza with Emmental (not mozzarella – *never* mozzarella) and a hard crust, wood-fired. Order the *moitié-moitié* – half anchovies, half cheese, a local classic – or go for a €2 slice and eat it standing up with everyone else. Pizza here isn't food; it's religion.

Near 93 boulevard de la Blancarde, 13004
Nearest metro: Cinq Avenues Longchamp

PIZZA CHEZ GE
AU FEU DE BOIS
06 48 03 90 97
FARINE

26
MOUTCHOU

The neighbourhood épicerie

Marseille's neighbourhoods were once separate villages before they got swallowed up by the city, and Endoume still feels like one – slow-paced, walkable and with small squares where everyone seems to know everyone. Moutchou calls itself the 'épicerie-café du village', and it lives up to that. You can eat soft-boiled eggs with good bread and butter for breakfast, grab lunch (often a delicious tarte), buy organic vegetables for dinner or pick up cheese for a raclette. You'll probably end up chatting to the locals about the Mistral while choosing tomatoes.

378 rue d'Endoume, 13007
Nearest bus stop: Endoume (line 83)
instagram.com/moutchou_epicerie

moutchou
ÉPICERIE CAFÉ

27

HAKO +

Marseille's calm corner

Fumio Ishikawa's tiny izakaya has barely a dozen seats, split between a windowed bar and one communal table. At lunch, you build your own bento: onigiri or rice, then five small dishes from whatever Fumio's made that day – perhaps fiery, crunchy vegetable tempura, eggs marinated in a rich soy broth or sashimi sliced to order. Or go for the daily special: often glazed teriyaki, which gives way to the city's creamiest ramen on Fridays and Saturdays (including a vegan option). Evening brings natural wine and small plates. The road outside never quiets down, but somehow this place stays in its own calm bubble.

218 Chemin du Roucas Blanc, 13007
Nearest bus stop: Le Terrail (lines 55, 73)
instagram.com/hakoplus13007

HAKO
HAKO°
OPEN

28
RAZZIA

The lunchtime raid

Rue Fontange has turned into one of Marseille's best food streets (see Caterine, no.8), and Razzia is part of why. They get their bread from Pain Pan down the road and pile it with things like sardine meatballs, crunchy fennel and cabbage with lemon mayo, or buttery green beans tossed with gribiche sauce. Lunch means a queue, but it moves fast – Thomas Benayoun pours coffee and chats while Axelle Poittevin works the kitchen. Don't skip dessert: maybe genmaicha cheesecake with figs, maybe something else entirely. Given the name, you'll want to grab one of everything.

2 rue Fontange, 13006
Nearest metro: Notre-Dame du Mont
instagram.com/razzia_marseille

29

MAISON EMPEREUR

Night at the hardware museum

Call something an institution too often and the word loses meaning, but Maison Empereur actually earns it. This family hardware shop in Noailles has been accumulating stuff since 1827. Tools, pots, brushes, panisses moulds: imagine it, and chances are it's here. Pop in for a screwdriver and you'll likely come out with a colander and a questioning look from your partner. For the full experience, book a night in the flat upstairs, surrounded by nearly 200 years of French craftsmanship, then head downstairs in the morning for a proper browse. Eventually you'll emerge back into bustling Noailles – but that's half the charm.

4 rue des Récolettes, 13001
Nearest metros: Noailles, Vieux-Port
empereur.fr

MAISON EMPEREUR
.4.
.4.

MPEREUR
la plus vieille
quincaillerie...
nichée au coeur
de Marseille

30

JOGGING

Former butcher's shop turned concept store

On Marseille's polished rue Paradis, the old *boucherie* sign is a perfect misdirection. Step inside and the contrast hits you: this is Jogging, the city's fashion nerve centre. Photographer Olivier Amsellem curates a sharp, expensive edit of Jacquemus and Lemaire, alongside limited-edition trainers and hard-to-find streetwear. His selection is so personal, it almost feels like an exhibition – pricey, yes, but a joy to browse. Walk through to the back and the mood softens, spilling into a leafy courtyard shaded by a huge tree. Here, the trattoria hosts rotating chefs serving modern Italian plates: turns out the city's best fashion shop is also great for lunch.

107 rue Paradis, 13006
Nearest metro: Estrangin
joggingjogging.com

31

SAVONNERIE MARSEILLAISE DE LA LICORNE

The real soap workshop

Forget the souvenir bars – this is where real Marseille soap comes to life. Serge Bruna still does it the old way, and you can watch him at work in his Cours Julien workshop. Regular free tours throughout the day (except Sundays) show you exactly how authentic savon de Marseille takes shape, complete with the satisfying thunk of soap blocks being cut. The fleur d'oranger (orange blossom) bars are the ones to buy, and since you're within walking distance of Saint-Charles station, they make excellent last-minute gifts. Just watch those steps if you've got luggage in tow.

34 Cours Julien, 13006
Nearest metros: Noailles, Notre-Dame du Mont
savon-de-marseille-licorne.com

32

SIMONELOO

The clay collector

Lou Thomas, the artist behind Simoneloo, is obsessed with texture. A two-month residency in Oaxaca, Mexico, had a profound impact on her style: she rarely uses glazes, preferring to let the raw clay speak for itself through deep grooves and wonderfully imperfect shapes. Her signature Bouboulita vases, a series of round-bellied forms inspired by Fernando Botero's paintings, are the perfect proof. Her studio, tucked behind a court-yard in a former mosaicist's workshop, is open by appointment (just send a DM on Instagram) – a rare chance to meet the artist in her space. Anyone interested in her work is welcomed, whether you're here to browse or buy direct from the source.

21 quai de la Joliette, 13002
Nearest metro: Joliette
instagram.com/simonelooceramics

33

ÉPICERIE L'IDÉAL

Stacked shelves and lunch

In the heart of the bustling Noailles market district, L'Idéal is a lesson in abundance. Julia Sammut's high-end grocery is gloriously crammed: bottles and tins stacked high, the deli counter overflowing with grilled artichokes in olive oil, caponata and portokalopita (Greek orange cake). Hot dishes come from the kitchen, but most people just point at the counter and take what looks good – with plenty of delicious vegan options. That quality comes at a price, but watch who else is shopping here; there's a reason half the chefs in Marseille come to l'Idéal.

11 rue d'Aubagne, 13001
Nearest metros: Noailles, Vieux-Port
epicerielideal.com

34

PROVISIONS

The makers' living room

Provisions is less a shop, more a clubhouse for people who care about how things are made. Jill Cousin and Saskia Porretta took over a three-generation-old bookshop and packed the wooden shelves with books on sustainability, small-batch wines and pantry staples that they hunt down on road trips. There's a weekly lunch menu, but the real magic is the constant rotation of events: anything from a pizza party for a cookbook launch to an exhibition of artisanal work shirts to a guest chef dinner. You'll walk in for a bottle of wine and leave having booked a two-day fermentation workshop.

95 rue de Lodi, 13006
Nearest metro: Baille
instagram.com/provisions.marseille

ANGLAIS
ITALIEN
ESPAGNOL
ALLE AND
ETC

35

LE PÈRE BLAIZE

Marseille's 200-year-old herbalist

Le Père Blaize has been here since 1815, curing hangovers, insomnia and god knows what else with plants. It started as folk healing, with mountain-herb knowledge passed down through the Blaize family. As France professionalised medicine in the 19th century, a new generation trained as pharmacists, blending inherited wisdom with modern science. The shop stayed in the family for six generations and is still run by a qualified pharmacist. Tell them what hurts and they'll make a custom remedy in the back – a reminder that 'natural' requires real expertise. The hours are erratic, but once you're in, stock up; the scent from the verbena tea alone will follow you down the street.

4 rue Méolan et du Père Blaize, 13001
Nearest metros: Noailles, Vieux-Port
pereblaize.fr

Bourrache
Genêt Fleurs
Cassis
Combretum
Lavande
Mauve bleue Fleurs
Maté
Uva-Ursi

36

ENAMOURA

The house of lights

Shopping for ceramic lamps probably isn't why you're in Marseille. But Enamoura, Magali Avignon's boutique atelier in the 6th arrondissement, might just change your mind. Magali designs lighting – curved terracotta pendants, textured stoneware sconces – that artisans handcraft in Provence. Book through the website and push through an unremarkable door, and you're in the *reserve*, where finished pieces crowd the shelves. Then Magali or her team walk you through the adjoining house, a beautifully styled space with lamps glowing in every room. Buy what you like, browse for ideas or just wander. And if you fall in love with the house itself? You can rent it for a holiday – all the details are online.

11 rue de Montévidéo, 13006
Nearest metro: Estrangin
enamoura.com

37

MAISON MÈRE

Kicks and collabs

Sneakerheads, this is your Marseille stop. Maison Mère stocks rare trainers tracked down across Europe and vintage streetwear that's hard to come by. But it's the collaborations that put them on the map, from limited drops with local musicians to cheeky projects with neighbourhood businesses. (A project with hip cheesemonger La Meulerie resulted in a t-shirt showing raclette cheese melting down a sneaker. Yes, really.) Beyond the shop, Maison Mère hosts a running club that loops through Marseille's streets – check Instagram to join.

5 rue Chevalier Roze, 13002
Nearest metro: Vieux-Port
maisonmere.eu

38

JIJI LA PALME D'OR

Colourful spices and homeware bazaar

Noailles is Marseille's belly – the cosmopolitan quarter where you can buy harissa at 9am and Tunisian pottery by lunch. In the maze of market stands and boutiques, Jiji stands out. Jihane Azizi took over her father's spice shop on rue d'Aubagne and expanded it into multiple storefronts facing each other across the street. One holds spices and dried fruits in glass jars, another hand-painted ceramics, another hand-blown glasses and wicker baskets. Somewhere in the mix, she's also squeezed in a hammam. The woman clearly doesn't sleep, but then again, neither does Noailles – maybe she's just feeding off the quarter's relentless buzz.

16 rue d'Aubagne, 13001
Nearest metro: Noailles
jijilapalmedor.com

PROMOTION
CACHE POT
140€ 130€
PROMOTION
PANIER
15€
PROMOTION
COUSSIN
29.90€
DOLCE
VITA
CIAO
ORE

39

SESSÙN ALMA

Fashion, food and found objects

Sessùn is one of Marseille's most celebrated fashion brands, founded here by Emma François after a trip to Guatemala sparked a love for textiles and indigenous crafts. Her concept store Alma sits in a former soap factory, all light and air under a massive glass roof. While the racks hold Sessùn's signature womenswear, the real focus here is what Emma loves: ceramics by Simoneloo (no.32) and other local makers, indie books, natural perfumes. There's a canteen at the front for coffee and seasonal lunches, with the boutique tucked in the back.

127 rue Sainte, 13007
Nearest metros: Estrangin, Vieux-Port
sessun.com

40

PAVILLON SOUTHWAY

Night at the gallery

Art historian Emmanuelle Luciani has pulled off a rare trick: creating a gallery–guesthouse in her 1880s villa that feels like a home, not a concept. The two bedrooms are installations you can sleep in – one draped in Mediterranean frescoes, the other all Gothic drama. The whole house is a showcase for the Southway Studio collective, with their work and rotating exhibitions in every room. Emmanuelle knows the city's art scene inside out, and her recommendations over breakfast are part of the deal. You're perfectly placed, too: Le Corbusier's Cité Radieuse (no.41) is a short walk away and the beaches are just down the road.

433 boulevard Michelet, 13009
Nearest bus stop: Obélisque (line B1)
southwaystudio.com

41

CITÉ RADIEUSE

Le Corbusier's vertical village

It might seem far away on a map, but this modernist landmark is worth the trek. Le Corbusier's 1950s vision of a self-contained 'vertical village' stacks apartments with shops, a restaurant and what he called 'interior streets'. The rooftop has a running track and paddling pool, plus MAMO, a former gym transformed by designer Ora-ïto into a contemporary art gallery with rotating installations. Check what's on before visiting as the opening hours shift with exhibitions. Want the full experience? Stay at Hôtel Le Corbusier inside, grab lunch at Le Ventre de l'Architecte, the retro-chic fine dining restaurant on the third floor, then roll on to Parc Borély (no.52) or the beach.

280 boulevard Michelet, 13008
Nearest metro: Rond-Point du Prado
citeradieuse-marseille.com

42

MUCEM

Marseille's cultural landmark

When Mucem landed on the waterfront in 2013, it did more than just give Marseille a world-class museum – it unlocked a whole part of the city. Rudy Ricciotti's design is a masterpiece: a black cube wrapped in concrete lace that filters the sunlight. Inside, the programming is just as bold, diving into every corner of Mediterranean culture from the history of football to the impact of gold. But the real masterstroke is the suspended footbridge linking this modern icon to the 17th-century Fort Saint-Jean, letting you drift between the cool galleries and the sun-drenched ramparts. For the grand finale, head to the rooftop, where three-star chef Alexandre Mazzia helms the restaurant.

7 promenade Robert Laffont, 13002
Nearest metro: Vieux-Port
mucem.org

43

FRICHE LA BELLE DE MAI

Arts hub in a former factory

The real energy in Marseille isn't down at the port – it's uphill, in the working-class grid of Belle de Mai, humming away inside this raw concrete arts complex. Artists took over the defunct tobacco factory in '92, and it has functioned as the neighbourhood's unofficial community centre ever since. Here, a skatepark shares space with experimental theatres and locals treat the gardens like their own backyard – especially when the Monday farmers' market rolls around. In summer, the whole place pivots to its massive rooftop terrace. Grab a beer, find a spot overlooking the railway tracks and watch the sun drop behind the city as a DJ starts to play.

41 rue Jobin, 13003
Nearest metro: Marseille Saint-Charles
Taxi recommended if travelling after dark
lafriche.org

44
LA VIEILLE CHARITÉ

Le Panier's baroque escape

Le Panier, Marseille's oldest neighbourhood, is a chaotic maze of steep alleys tangled with laundry lines and tourists. For a dose of calm, duck into this 17th-century almshouse. Pierre Puget designed la Vieille Charité for Marseille's poor, and the pink stone arcades wrapping around the chapel still carry that quiet dignity. After the war, the city wanted to tear it down, but Le Corbusier convinced them otherwise. Now, it houses Mediterranean archaeology upstairs and contemporary exhibitions below, and something about those baroque bones makes modern work sharper. The courtyard cafe, OLLā, is there when you need to sit and take it all in.

2 rue de la Charité, 13002
Nearest metros: Colbert, Jules Guesde
vieille-charite-marseille.com

45

FRICHE DE L'ESCALETTE

Summer sculpture park at land's end

Out where Marseille starts to run out of road, art collector Éric Touchaleaume has claimed the ruins of a 19th-century lead factory. He dropped Jean Prouvé's modernist pavilions right into the crumbling stone and scattered contemporary sculpture across a site where the only backdrop is the white cliffs of the Calanques. It's a strange, compelling mix, and you only have July and August to see it up close as it's closed the rest of the year. If you find the gates locked, don't despair: the coastal path above is a brilliant walk in its own right and you can catch glimpses of the sculptures from the clifftop. Plus, you're just around the corner from a drink at Tuba (no.57).

route des Goudes, impasse de l'Escalette, 13008
Getting there: car/taxi recommended
friche-escalette.com

46
TALUS TIERS-LIEU

The cemetery's lively neighbour

Leave it to Marseille to put one of its best green spaces right next to a cemetery. Le Talus is an urban farm built on an old dump beside Saint-Pierre and, for a city short on parks, it's become essential. By day, it's a relaxed jumble of vegetable plots, a chicken coop and wooden tables for vegetarian lunches. Come summer, Friday nights turn into a *guinguette* – which is just the old French way of saying open-air party. Local bands play, the wine flows and half the neighbourhood turns up to dance. The mostly residential 12th arrondissement doesn't get enough love, but this place is changing that.

603–623 rue Saint-Pierre, 13012
Nearest metro: La Timone
instagram.com/letalusmarseille

EXPERTS AUTOS SERVICES

47

LE COUVENT

The convent's second act

If you needed more proof that the district of Belle de Mai runs Marseille's art scene, here it is. This former convent now houses 80 artists across 40 studios, with two converted chapels for exhibitions. It's a hive of activity: the calendar is packed with concerts and workshops and in summer the gardens come to life for communal meals. It's wilder and more open than a traditional arts centre – you can wander through during the day, see a concert at night or join a session. The whole point is that everyone is welcome.

52 rue Levat, 13003
Nearest metro: Marseille Saint-Charles
Taxi recommended if travelling after dark
le-couvent.org

TINA
CHARLY
TINA
CHARLY

48

NOTRE-DAME DE LA GARDE

Where sailors say thank you

Marseillais call her la Bonne Mère (the Good Mother) and she's been standing guard over the city since the 1860s. The golden statue of the Virgin Mary holding baby Jesus sits atop the basilica, and you'll spot her the moment you arrive at Saint-Charles train station. Inside, the walls are covered with ex-votos: plaques and model boats thanking her for bringing sailors home safely and protecting families. You can hike up if you're feeling ambitious (it's steep) or take the bus, but the petit train is more fun (buy tickets from the booth on quai du Port). Once you're up there, you'll see what makes her so special – the view takes in all of Marseille, spread out below like it's always been hers to protect.

rue Fort du Sanctuaire, 13006
Getting there: 1 min walk from
Notre-Dame de la Garde (bus) or take petit train
basiliquenotredamedelagarde.com

CAPITAINERIE

49

PORT DE L'ESTAQUE

The port locals keep secret

You've done Les Calanques, you've walked La Corniche. Now head north to L'Estaque, where Marseille drops the postcard act. Yes, Cézanne painted those red roofs tumbling down to the sea, but forget the art history for a moment. There's no tourist polish here – the harbour bustles with working fishermen and the only queue you'll find is for Chez Magali's panisses. These golden chickpea fritters are worth the trip alone – crispy, salty and served scalding hot in paper cones. Grab a spot by the water and soak up a scene that hasn't changed much since the painters packed up their easels. Jump on a coastal train (which takes just seven minutes from central Marseille) or catch the €5 ferry from Vieux-Port (April–September).

Port de L'Estaque, 13016
Nearest train station: L'Estaque

50

CALANQUES DE LA CÔTE BLEUE

The quieter coastal gems

While everyone obsesses over the national park's more famous calanques, locals quietly slip away to the Côte Bleue. And so should you. These calanques west of the city have the same dramatic coastline – without the summer access restrictions – just with fewer tourists and more Marseillais escaping the heat. The train from Saint-Charles to Niolon is half the fun – a slow-motion coastal ride through viaducts and tunnels that feels like a movie set. Walk the seaside trail from Niolon to La Redonne if you want the full experience or just grab lunch at La Pergola on Niolon's tiny port and swim off the rocks.

Nearest train station: Niolon

51

CHÂTEAU D'IF

Formidable citadel off the coast

Fiction made the Château d'If famous. This former prison was long thought to have held the Man in the Iron Mask – a 17th-century political prisoner whose identity has never been revealed – as well as being a setting in Alexandre Dumas's *The Count of Monte Cristo*. The 16th-century fortress sits on a rocky island between Marseille and the Frioul archipelago, a 20-minute ferry ride from Vieux-Port (the same boat that goes to Frioul, no.53). Visit to examine centuries of graffiti carved into the castle walls – though note that crossings get cancelled when the Mistral picks up, and once you see those waves hitting the rocks, you'll understand why no one ever successfully escaped.

Getting there: 20 min ferry from Vieux-Port
frioul-if-express.com

52
LE PARC BORÉLY

Where Marseille goes green

Marseille does blue brilliantly. It does rugged cliffs and coastal trails. But green urban space? Not so much. Enter Parc Borély: this 17-hectare oasis near the Prado beaches gives the city room to breathe. French gardens spread out in front of the château, English paths loop the lake and there's even a Chinese garden courtesy of Shanghai. Rent a rosalie (four-wheeled pedal cars that families love) or just stroll the lake watching kids feed ducks. The château holds a small but good museum, there's a cafe for refuelling and a path that leads straight to the beach when you're done.

avenue du Parc Borély, 13008
Nearest bus stop: Parc Borély (lines 19, 83)

53
FRIOUL ISLANDS

Marseille's offshore escape

The Frioul islands sit 4 km offshore, watching the city from the horizon, yet somehow most visitors never make the crossing. The 30-minute ferry drops you somewhere that feels stuck in time – Port du Frioul is ramshackle in the best way, home to around a hundred residents living among buildings that haven't changed in a while. Turn right from the port; Ratonneau island's coastal path takes you past beautiful coves and 19th-century hospital ruins (the island was used to quarantine plague ships). Or cross the dyke to Pomègues island for longer hikes and hidden beaches. In summer, the last ferry back leaves at 10pm: plenty of time for a glass of rosé by the water.

Getting there: 30 min ferry from Vieux-Port
frioul-if-express.com

54
PARC NATIONAL DES CALANQUES
Your edge-of-the-map playground

Ah, les Calanques. The pride and joy of locals – though they're technically shared with neighbouring towns Cassis and La Ciotat, but let's not get sidetracked. These limestone coves carved into the Mediterranean coast are everything the postcards promise and more. They are beautiful by boat, but hiking puts you right in the middle of it all. Bus B1 gets you to Luminy (the trailhead for Sugiton calanque), while other lines reach Sormiou and Morgiou coves. Access is often restricted in the summer months due to wildfire risk, so come off-season when you'll have them more to yourself. Pack plenty of water and sturdy shoes and be ready for steep, rocky paths.

Getting there: various access points,
check website for details
calanques-parcnational.fr

55

LES COLLINES DE MARSEILLE PAGNOL

Pagnol's childhood playground

Marcel Pagnol – writer, filmmaker and Marseille's favourite son – spent his childhood roaming these limestone hills east of the city. His autobiographical novels, *My Father's Glory* and *My Mother's Castle*, both published in 1957, turned the Garlaban massif into legend, and these days the trails are known as the Pagnol hills. There are dozens of routes to choose from, ranging from easy walks through the scrubland to challenging summit hikes. Le Garlaban, at 714 metres, is the most ambitious – the views from the top stretch across Marseille, the valley below and out to the sea. Check access before you go in summer; the massif closes when fire risk climbs.

Trailheads start from La Treille, Aubagne and Allauch
Getting there: 20–30 minutes by car/taxi

56

MALMOUSQUE

The city's quiet cove

Just past the Vallon des Auffes – the famous fishing cove with a postcard-perfect bridge – lies Malmousque, the smaller, scrappier sibling. Here, a maze of tiny alleys spits you out onto a miniature port and a coastline of sun-baked rocks. In summer, the whole neighbourhood treats it like a beach, jumping straight into the deep, clear water. Even when it's busy, there's always a patch of dry stone to claim for your towel and the pan bagnat (a niçoise salad sandwich) you grabbed from Cécile (no.5) up the hill. But winter is the sweet spot, when the rocks empty out and you finally have space for a quiet sunset with a bottle of wine.

Anse de Malmousque, 13007
Nearest bus stop: Endoume (line 83)

57

TUBA CLUB

Cliffside refuge with a waiting list

You've probably seen those yellow striped loungers perched on the rocks on Instagram, overlooking endless blue. Yes, it's expensive and you have to book well ahead, but Tuba Club earns the hype. Tucked into the rocky coastline at Les Goudes, this former diving club keeps fun reminders of its underwater past, right down to the industrial-looking pipes and valve wheels in the showers. The original rooms are small and stylish, and close to the lively restaurant, but the newer suites are spacious (if you're in the mood to splurge). When the weather plays ball, linger in Bikini – the rooftop cocktail bar, also open to non-guests – and don't miss Sylvain Roucayrol's menu: it goes bright and briny with pristine sashimi and sharp Mediterranean plates.

2 boulevard Alexandre Delabre, 13008
Getting there: car/taxi recommended
tuba-club.com

58

LES BORDS DE MER

Art Deco elegance on the Corniche

Perched right on the Corniche, Marseille's scenic coastal road, this gleaming Art Deco hotel has just 19 rooms, all facing the Mediterranean. You're so close to the water you might as well be on a boat – only with better food and a subterranean spa dug into the rock. The rooftop pool overlooks the sea but staying here also gets you into the Cercle des Nageurs across the bay – the city's most exclusive swimming club. It's usually off-limits, but guests can use the Olympic pool and the rocky creek alongside the impossibly tanned regulars.

52 Corniche Président John Fitzgerald Kennedy, 13007
Nearest bus stop: Corniche Dessemond (line 83)
lesbordsdemer.fontenille-collection.com

59

VILLA MEDJÉ

A vintage hideaway above the sea

You have to earn this place – the climb up from the Corniche is no joke, but the view makes it irrelevant. Pénélope Comet has turned this old house into a riot of colour and vintage soul, hunting down every piece of furniture to create an artistic sanctuary. You book the whole two-bedroom property, so it's just you, the sweeping sea views and a garden that sometimes hosts events. Staying here is like borrowing the keys from your coolest friend – if your friend lived in the perfect house above the Mediterranean.

15 traverse de la Baudille, 13007
Nearest bus stop: Vallon de la Baudille (line 83)
villamedje.fr

TROPICAL

60

GRAND JUSTE

The hotel Notre-Dame-du-Mont deserved

The central neighbourhood of Notre-Dame-du-Mont has always been the place to go out, but never the place to stay. Grand Juste finally balances the equation. It's bafflingly quiet given you're minutes from the busy Cours Julien district (and Mercato, no.68), feeling less like a hotel and more like a sanctuary. The rooms are stylish and well-designed, but the real win is the garden out back. Ignore the breakfast menu, grab a free coffee and take it outside while the streets are still hushed. It's the perfect base: close enough to stumble home, peaceful enough to recover.

80 rue Auguste Blanqui, 13005
Nearest metro: Notre-Dame du Mont
justejuste.com

61

HÔTEL AMISTA

Noailles in technicolour

Behind a classic 19th-century facade of lion heads and wrought iron, the former Hôtel Saint-Louis has reinvented itself. Designer Dorothée Delaye has turned the volume up, filling the rooms with an explosion of colour that matches the energy of Noailles, the city's vibrant market quarter. It's a mix of patterned fabrics, eclectic furniture and the warmth of a Provençal home. You're in the thick of the action, so skip the dining room and head straight for the stalls as they open or cross the street to Pétrin Couchette (no.10).

2 rue des Récolettes, 13001
Nearest metros: Noailles, Vieux-Port
hotel-amista-marseille.fr

AMISTA
Maison Provençale · 1884

62

LA CARAVELLE

Jazz and cocktails above the port

La Caravelle has held the high ground on Vieux-Port for decades, perched on the first floor above the harbour-front bustle. Most people climb the stairs for the balcony – it's tiny, with just a handful of tables facing Notre-Dame de la Garde (no.48) – but the real atmosphere is inside. Under the low ceilings, the zinc bar hosts jazz bands on Wednesdays and Fridays, pulling in locals who come for the music, not the scenery. It's wood-panelled, slightly worn, and has been here since the 1930s, outlasting most of the bars in the city.

34 quai du Port, 13002
Nearest metro: Vieux-Port
lacaravelle-marseille.com

HOTEL
BELLE-VUE
LA CARAVELLE
Le GRAND COMPTOIR de Paris
A emporter ~ take away
LE COMPTOIR BELLE VUE
HOTEL BELLEVUE
32

63

FARE L'AMORE

Love at first spritz

Italian Chiara Brunone and French Stan Boulanger brought their love story to a quiet corner of Endoume and promptly turned it into the neighbourhood's liveliest party. Inside, a huge round counter pulls everyone in for Negronis; outside, the massive terrace commands the junction. For a few hours each evening, you could be in Rome. The air is full of vintage Italian music, and the only things that seem to matter are the next round of Aperol Spritzes and another plate of burrata. Stick around past 10pm, and the civilised aperitivo gives way to an all-out fiesta.

45 rue Paul Codaccioni, 13007
Nearest bus stop: Place du 4 Septembre (lines 54, 81)
farelamoremarseille.com

RIZZI
LA CUCINA
VEGETALINE

64

LE CABANON DE PAULETTE

Rosé and tapas on the sand

This place is an homage to 'mamie' (grandma) Paulette, who used to cook for friends on this tiny beach. Today, the place lives on in the same old boat garages, with a concrete terrace of tables so close to the water that you could almost dip your toes in. Come for a sunset apéro of rosé and panisses or book ahead via DM for the moules-frites with aioli. It's summer-only, cash-only and a cab ride out, but none of that matters once you're here with your feet up and a glass in hand.

boulevard des Baigneurs, 13008
Getting there: car/taxi recommended
instagram.com/lecabanondepaulette

Paulette

65

DÉRIVE

Marseille's cocktail newcomer

Not so long ago, the city's cocktail scene wasn't much to write home about. That's changing fast, and Dérive is leading the charge. Just off Plage des Catalans, this is the kind of place that makes you want to extend your beach day. Here, the classics are made properly – or tweaked when inspiration strikes – and there's good craft beer if that's your thing. The blue-and-green-tiled space suits the seaside vibe, and chef Anne Leplumey's panisses always hit the spot. Even better? The low and no-alcohol options aren't an afterthought, including seasonal kombuchas made in Marseille.

51 rue de Suez, 13007
Nearest bus: Le Pharo (lines 82s, 83)
instagram.com/derive_marseille

66

LE CAFÉ DE L'ABBAYE

Sunset drinks by the railing

The nightly ritual at Café de l'Abbaye starts when the sun begins to drop behind Saint-Victor Abbey. First, the few tables are claimed, then more seem to appear from nowhere. When they're gone, the crowd crosses to the stone wall overlooking the port, drinks perched on the ledge, watching the sky turn orange. It's a simple, unpretentious spot that runs on its own schedule – order your cheap beer or natural wine at the bar, hope they've made panisses and stay until the last person decides to call it a night. No reservations, obviously.

3 rue d'Endoume, 13007
Nearest metro: Vieux-Port
*instagram.com/le_cafe_de_labbaye_*

CAFE DE L'ABBAYE
RICARD
RICARD
Entreprise BEGA

67

LE CHAPITEAU

Belle de Mai's open-air party

Marseille loves a hybrid space, and Le Chapiteau might be the city's best attempt at it. This sprawling 2,700-square-metre open-air club in Belle de Mai is built entirely from reclaimed materials, right down to the pallet furniture. One minute you're playing pétanque, the next you're grabbing pizza, then you're on a dancefloor with international DJs. The atmosphere is refreshingly unpretentious: inclusive, safe and more about the music than the posturing. Forget the velvet rope; this is just a very good party.

38 traverse Notre-Dame de Bon Secours, 13003
Nearest bus stop: Belle de Mai Loubon
(lines 33, 34, 49, 56, 533, 582)
Taxi recommended if travelling after dark
lechapiteau-marseille.fr

68

MERCATO

Football and natural wine

The name? Football, obviously. Mercato is the player transfer window – a perfect fit for a city that lives and breathes Olympique de Marseille. One wall here is covered in the team's scarves, an Arsenal scarf tucked among them. Fred Semerdjian runs Mercato from behind the bar, sometimes cooking, sometimes hosting guest chefs. The menu shifts constantly but you can expect layers of spice and sweetness, like feta borek laced with honey, paper-thin lahmajoun (spiced lamb flatbread) with a charred crust, or silky taramasalata. What never changes is the wine: Fred's built one of the best natural wine lists in Marseille. The space is all concrete but not cold – probably because Fred's there pouring for a room that keeps filling up.

36 rue de la Loubière, 13006
Nearest metro: Notre-Dame du Mont
instagram.com/mercato_winesucker

69

LA RELÈVE

Where Endoume gathers for apéro

Why would you choose a bar on a loud, traffic-filled road? Because it's La Relève, and that's where everyone is. Every evening, the terrace is packed, with the *apéro* crowd spilling onto the pavement. What starts with a glass of pastis often stretches into the night as people dig in, refusing to leave. The bar has been an institution since 1944, and the new owners kept the old-school shell of tiles and zinc while bringing fresh energy to the place. For those who don't want the night to end, there are four colourful, '50s-inspired guest rooms upstairs.

41 rue d'Endoume, 13007
Nearest metro: Estrangin
larelevemarseille.fr

BAR
2026
JANVIER

70
BARTA

Winter clubbing by the sea

Marseille's nightlife has a reputation for dying outside of summer, when the beach clubs close and good options get scarce. Le Barta was born to fight that. Run by the team behind one of the city's best-loved summer spots, La Cabane des Amis, this club by the sea keeps the energy going year-round. Expect hip-hop, reggaeton, Afro house and melodic techno three nights a week that run until the early hours. It's proof that Marseille doesn't have to shut down when winter hits.

83 avenue de la Pointe Rouge, 13008
Getting there: car/taxi recommended
instagram.com/barta.marseille

BARTA

71

LA DAME NOIR

Where Marseille goes to dance

You wouldn't expect to find one of the city's best clubs in a former naval complex, but that's Marseille for you. Le Trolleybus is a sprawling venue by Vieux-Port with multiple rooms, but La Dame Noir is the standout. Every weekend, a line-up of DJs spins house, disco and techno to a packed floor of people who are there for one reason: to dance. It's a genuine, sweaty club night that goes until dawn – phones stay in pockets and the music does the rest.

24 quai de Rive Neuve, 13007
Nearest metro: Vieux-Port
instagram.com/letrolley

IMAGE CREDITS

Page 2 © Delaney Inamine; page 4 © Lenor Lumineau; page 5 © Maxime Verre, photo, Building © Architects Rudy Ricciotti & Roland Carta, image courtesy Mucem; page 6 © Mickaël A. Bandassak; page 7 © Anne Claire Heraud; page 8 © Maximilian Müller; Sépia © Sépia; Limmat © Lenor Lumineau; Livingston © Franck Menegaux; Poissonnerie Kennedy © Fabien Voileau; La Marine des Goudes © La Marine des Goudes; Cécile Food Club © Cécile Food Club / fcclap; Ourea © Caroline Dutrey; Caterine ©Leo Kharfan; Le Four des Navettes © Helene Roche Photography; Pétrin Couchette © Adrian Bautista; Chez Yassine © Leo Kharfan; La Ola © La Ola; Île Degaby © Mickaël A. Bandassak; Bistrot Sassy © Bistrot Sassy; Bistrot Baya © Leo Kharfan; Bouillabaisse Turfu © Leo Kharfan; Boulangerie Merlin © Leo Kharfan; Sur Le Pouce © Leo Kharfan; Chez Étienne © Leo Kharfan; La Cantinetta © Philippe Conti; Prosper © Mickael Bandassak; Au Contraire Pâtisserie © Au Contraire Pâtisserie; Chez Petit Jean © Chez Petit Jean; Chez Moe © Leo Bourdin; Pizza Truck Chez Gé © Leo Bourdin; Moutchou © Leo Kharfan; Hako + © Leo Kharfan; Razzia © Leo Kharfan; Maison Empereur © Fred Tchalekian, @fredtchalekian; Jogging © Jogging; Savonnerie Marseillaise de la Licorne © Savonnerie Marseillaise de la Licorne; Simoneloo © Richard Ducros; Épicerie L'Idéal © Leo Kharfan; Provisions ©Louise Skadhauge; Le Père Blaize © Père Blaize; Enamoura ©Adel Fecih; Maison Mère © Maison Mère; Jiji La Palme d'Or © Suzanne Desplanques; Sessùn Alma © Victoria Nossent; Pavillon Southway © Adel Fecih; Cité Radieuse © Chris Hellier; Mucem © Maxime Verre, photo, Building © Architects Rudy Ricciotti & Roland Carta, image courtesy Mucem; Friche la Belle de Mai © Caroline Dutrey; La Vieille Charité © Olivier Rateau; Friche de l'Escalette © Friche de L'Escalette, Galerie 54, Paris; Talus Tiers-Lieu © Alban Besson; Le Couvent © Romain Pottier; Notre-Dame de la Garde first image © Luri Buriak, second image © Aterrom; Port de L'Estaque first image © Gacro 74, second image © Hemis; Calanques de la Côte Bleu first image © Gacro 74, second image © Hemis; Château d'If © Patricia Phillips; Le Parc Borély © Olivier Rateau; Frioul Islands first image © Jean-Luc Ichard, second image © Hemis; Parc National des Calanques © Christopher Shoults; Les Collines de Marseille Pagnol © Hemis; Malmousque © Abaca Press; Tuba Club first image © Delaney Inamine, following images © Edouard Sanville; Les Bords de Mer © Stephane Abourdaram / WE ARE CONTENTS; Villa Medjé © Villa Medjé; Grand Juste © Solasta Production; Hôtel Amista © Pierre Monetta; La Caravelle © Leo Kharfan; Fare L'Amore © Fare L'Amore; Le Cabanon de Paulette © Hemis; Dérive © Enzo Arrus and Maelle Lemen; Le Café de l'Abbaye ©Yama @ frnkfrtr; Le Chapiteau © Jeremy Teller; Mercato © Leo Kharfan; La Relève © Leo Kharfan; Barta © Terrace OFC; La Dame Noir © Lucie Pix @luciefstudio.

An Opinionated Guide to Marseille
First edition, first printing

Published in 2026 by Hoxton Mini Press, London.
Copyright © Hoxton Mini Press 2026. All rights reserved.
Text © Sandrine Faure 2026.

Text by Sandrine Faure
Editing by Florence Ward
Production Design by Dom Grant
Production Control by David Brimble
Proofreading by Gaynor Sermon
Editorial support by Richard Enright

With thanks to Matthew Young for
initial series design.

Please note: we recommend checking the
websites listed for each entry before you
visit for the latest information on price,
opening times and pre-booking
requirements.

The right of Sandrine Faure to be
identified as the author of the text has
been asserted under the Copyright,
Designs and Patents Act 1988.

Thank you to all of the individuals and
institutions who have provided images
and arranged permissions. While every
effort has been made to trace the present
copyright holders we apologise in advance
for any unintentional omission or error,
and would be pleased to insert the
appropriate acknowledgement in any
subsequent edition.

No part of this publication may be
reproduced, stored in a retrieval system,
or transmitted in any form or by any
means, electronic, mechanical,
photocopying, recording or otherwise,
without the prior written permission of
the copyright owner.

A CIP catalogue record for this book is
available from the British Library.

ISBN: 978-1-917719-14-8

Printed and bound by OZGraf, Poland

Manufacturer: Hoxton Mini Press, 104
Northside Studios, 16–29 Andrews Road,
London E8 4QF, UK
www.hoxtonminipress.com

Represented by: Authorised Rep
Compliance Ltd., Ground Floor, 71 Lower
Baggot Street, Dublin D02 P593, Ireland
www.arccompliance.com

Hoxton Mini Press is an environmen-
tally conscious publisher, committed
to offsetting our carbon footprint.
This book is 100 per cent carbon
compensated, with offset purchased
from Stand For Trees.

Every time you order from our website, we
plant a tree: www.hoxtonminipress.com

Selected opinionated guides in the series:
For more go to www.hoxtonminipress.com

ABOUT HOXTON MINI PRESS

Hoxton Mini Press is a small indie publisher based in east London. We make beautiful books with a dedication to sustainable production and great photography.

When we started the company, people told us print was dead; we wanted to prove them wrong. Books are no longer just about information, but objects to collect and own.

We promise three things. Firstly, nothing in this guidebook is sponsored; it's our own independent opinion. Secondly, our books are 100 per cent carbon compensated with printing, paper and transport fully offset. And finally, everything is researched, edited and written by humans, not AI.

INDEX